To: MICAEL
from Liesjé

UNPLANNED ODYSSEY

A memoir of wartime survival

Elisabeth H. "Liesje" Wilson
As told to Roy F. Wilson

iUniverse, Inc.
New York   Bloomington

Unplanned Odyssey
A memoir of wartime survival

iUniverse books may be ordered through booksellers or by contacting:

iUniverse
1663 Liberty Drive
Bloomington, IN 47403
www.iuniverse.com
1-800-Authors (1-800-288-4677)

ISBN: 978-1-4401-2409-9 (pbk)
ISBN: 978-1-4401-2410-5 (ebk)

Library of Congress Control Number: 2009923037

Printed in the United States of America

iUniverse rev. date: 02/27/2009

DEDICATION

I dedicate this book to the unknown strangers who sheltered me when I was a concentration camp escapee on the run; to the courageous staff of the birthing clinic in Jakarta who turned away the Kempei-tai officer who sought my infant son; to stalwart Mrs. Boerboom who cared for my son through my months in prison, and sheltered us again in the unsettled months after Japan's defeat; to the friends who supported me through the difficult years in Japan afterwards, and finally; to all the suffering innocents throughout the world, human beings reduced to the abstract statistic; "collateral damage," when nations go to war.

ACKNOWLEDGEMENTS

This book would not have been possible without the encouragement of many friends who have pushed me, some gently and others persistently, for years to tell my story. They have urged me, rightly so, to not only pass it along to the next generations in my family, but also to tell the world of those times in the Pacific Theatre as seen and experienced by one of the millions of "collaterals" who are inevitably affected by the war.

I am deeply indebted to and grateful to my husband, Roy Wilson, my love of nearly sixty years. He reached out to me in one of my most troubled times in Japan as a "gaijin" (foreigner), and has been a constant friend, companion and husband since, giving me new hope and a new life in America. He helped me recall and articulate my memories, molding my words into a coherent whole, which he lovingly recorded for me on these pages.

I am also indebted to Sumiko Meguro, a dear Japanese friend, who helped me realize that the intersection of my world with the pre-War world of my ex-husband, Sakai, had a profound and independent impact on him. Sumiko

vii

interviewed me more than ten years ago for background on an article she was preparing for publication in Japan, titled, "War and Love - A letter to Roy-chan". Roy-chan is Sakai's and my son. Sumiko's perspective more strongly emphasized Sakai's noble Samurai family, their role in Japanese history, and his life after we were divorced, showing the personal conflicts he went through as the old Samurai way struggled to survive in a new postwar world. I do hope her article was published in Japan. Though English is not her native language, she made a great effort to provide a translation, which Roy edited. We are grateful for her effort, and it allowed us to appreciate her different focus.

Here, I have presented my personal, as-lived and survived experiences, as I remember them, in my own words.

Liesje Wilson
As told to my husband, Roy Wilson
Sequim, Washington
January 2009

INTRODUCTION

By
Roy F. Wilson

This story begins in Batavia, Java, N.E.I. N.E.I. stood for "Netherlands East Indies." The place is still there, and the island is still called "Java," but the city is called Jakarta now, and the country is Indonesia.

The change of names reflects the rise and fall of empires in the defining events of the twentieth century. This story is the recollection of a woman caught up in those events. Battered and mauled by forces beyond her control, she survived.

The document recording her birth was impressive; two legal-size sheets of stiff paper, watermarked with the Dutch coat of arms, written in the Dutch language, slathered with official stamps, grommeted and tied with red tape. The original was lost in a life of many moves, and today only an English translation remains.

The language is stilted, a literal translation of the original. It reads: "FRANCISCUS JOHANNES

GERHARDUS MEIJER, age 21, occupation: Sergeant first Class, residing with Master CORNELIS, who is now present. Mr. MEIJER has informed me that at 2100 hours, 21 Feb. 22, in the military hospital at WELTEVREDEN in BATAVIA, his wife Wilhelmina Nuijen, no occupation, living with said Mr. MEIJER, gave birth to a female child, given name, Elisabeth Hennriette Anna. This document was drawn up in the presence of Hijman FRANANHUIS, age 30, occupation: Sgt. Major Administrator, Infantry; and Christiaan Edwin LINGER, age 26, occupation: Sgt. First Class, Infantry, both residing with Master CORNELIS who is now present.

This act is herewith concluded and, having been read and properly represented, is duly subscribed to by the registrant, the two witnesses and myself."

Below these words on the original document were the florid signatures of the father, the two witnesses and the registrar, identified as S.P. PIEROLIE.

The signatures and official stamps of no less than four layers of higher officials, up to the Secretary of the Department of Justice of the Netherlands Indies, further attest to this event.

It seems a lot of pomp for the simple act it records, but it was the way of the Dutch bureaucracy then. It assures us that a baby girl named Elisabeth was indeed born at the indicated time and place.

The lives and fates of the witnesses and officials attesting to this matter are lost in the passage of time, but in ensuing years, Sgt. Meijer trained in chemistry and pharmacology. A man of singular drive and determination, he rose through the ranks to become a commissioned officer in the Dutch army. But his drive and determination did not always benefit his personal life, and the lives of those around him.

Liesje's Father, Frans Meijer – 1923

Capt. Meijer completed his military career, and retired just before World War II. Recalled to active service when the war began, he was captured with his fellow Dutch soldiers when the Japanese invaded. Transported to a prisoner-of-war camp in northern Japan, his medical training helped many of his fellow prisoners survive.

Those soldiers from the Indies, clad in the rags of worn out tropical uniforms, were forced to work in coalmines in a land of harsh winters. Ill-fed, ill-housed, ill-clothed, overworked, subjected daily to brutality and contempt from their Japanese captors, many succumbed. Capt. Meijer survived and returned to his home after the war to retire once more.

In the years between, the world turned many times, and the old life was gone. The Indonesian people revolted against the Dutch, and the Department of Justice of the Netherlands Indies that solemnized Elisabeth's birth, ceased to exist. The nation became Indonesia, and the city called Batavia, became Jakarta. But the old hospital building where Liesje was born, built like a fortress, is there today. If nothing else, those Dutch colonials built strong.

I just called Elisabeth, "Liesje." It is a nickname. Translated to English, it means something like "Little Lizzie." "Liesje" has a nicer sound. It will be the name she uses throughout this tale.

Captain Meijer's own life went by twists and turns as the tides of change swept through his adopted homeland, and in 1957, Indonesian politics compelled his return to Holland. His life is a story in itself but this is Liesje's tale.

The little girl, whose birth is recorded here, began life as a colonial occupier in a subjugated land. Cosseted and comforted by maids, houseboys, cooks and chauffeurs, her life became by turns idyllic, tragic, and brutal. It led her ultimately to Japan where we met and married while I was in military service, and finally to the United States where we have lived for more than fifty years.

Her story, as she recalls it now, begins below.

Roy F. Wilson
Sequim, Washington
January 2009

PROLOGUE

I'm 86 years old. Unpleasant things happened to me in my early life; wartime experiences shared by few, which may seem incomprehensible by many today. My children, my grandchildren, and my great-grandchildren have heard references to this past, but none have heard the whole story. Only the eldest, Roy Jr., experienced any of the things that went before our arrival in America.

These events happened long ago, and I put them out of my mind. As I age, memories of the unpleasantness have returned to trouble me. I ponder the question of how, and why I survived those years, but I find no answer.

Without direct experience, my descendants cannot comprehend the reality of war, or what I went through in my youth, in order to survive and become their ancestor. I am driven to tell them, and I have written this story so they may know.

The Japanese, perhaps understandably, would like to expunge from the historical record, certain aspects of their wartime behavior. I wish I could expunge it from my memory, as well, but the unpleasant events I experienced were at their hands. I hold no grudge against the Japanese people, and never did, but I still do not understand how the Japanese culture could countenance their wartime policies, and the behavior of certain individuals I encountered.

This story takes us through my youth, my experiences in Indonesia in World War II, and in Japan through the immediate postwar years. I stopped at the point I sailed from Japan to America with my present husband, and two of our children.

Fifty-six years have passed since then, and I've lived a full life. Those fifty-six years also make a tale worth telling, but at age eighty-six, I don't have time left to tell it.

CHAPTER I
THE PREWAR YEARS

I remember heat; Indonesia straddles the equator. I knew nothing different until I was seven. I was cared for by nannies, we had a cook, a chauffeur, maids, and houseboys. I remember watching my parents dressing for social affairs, and how beautiful I thought my mother was.

I remember living in different cities as my father, Frans, was transferred to new military assignments in places with names like Medan, Padang, Semarang, Bandung, Salatiga, and Banda Aceh, (A tsunami destroyed that city in 2004).

I remember making friends and losing them as my family was transferred about, and I remember my mother getting sick.

The tropical climate was a hardship for many Europeans, but I'm told my parents both adjusted well. Life for the Dutch colonials was good. Work was finished in the cool morning hours, afternoons were spent relaxing and socializing, and servants were there to care for every need.

I'm told that from the outset my mother's health was frail. After I was born, in quick succession, she bore two more daughters, Johanna (Jopy), and Antonia (Toni). The stress sapped her vitality; she contracted tuberculosis, and went into a tuberculosis sanitarium in the city of Semarang.

My Family – 1926

I was four years old then, and of the three girls only I have clear memories of her. My lasting image is of her racking cough, and a handkerchief she carried to collect the phlegm she spit up.

There were other stresses on Wilhelmina. I remember events I didn't understand, and I heard secret whisperings. With a child's sensitivity, I knew something serious was happening that was not my business. Years later, in conversations with family members I pieced together a tale of abandonment and infidelity.

My father Frans, an intense man and a strict disciplinarian, had a violent temper that could quickly spill over onto us children. As the eldest, I was supposed to be the example, so I often bore the brunt of his temper. Only once did I see violence directed toward my mother.

Long after I left home, I learned that my father was a man driven to succeed, and he pursued his educational and career goals with a zeal that led him to neglect his wife and family. He encouraged his wife to seek social contacts elsewhere, and she had an affair, certainly an unintended consequence, but one that could have been predicted. I don't know what anguish the man may have suffered, and I don't know if he realized his own neglect led to it.

I remember vividly our last meeting with my mother. I was five. She wore a dress of white chiffon with a pattern of poppies, daisies and bachelor buttons, and she carried a broad-brimmed white hat with a red ribbon. She was beautiful, and I didn't understand why we couldn't stay together.

At the end she hugged and kissed the three of us, one by one, and gave each a kewpie doll, some candy, and chocolates. She turned, waved goodbye, and returned to the sanitarium. We never saw her again.

I wonder today at her feelings about losing us. Twice in the most difficult time of my life, I could have lost my son. I don't believe I could have tolerated what she went through, and I wonder about that final separation. Was it truly the product of her tuberculosis, or did it result from the split between my parents? All who could answer that question are gone.

My Family – 1929

In 1929, when I was seven, our father took us to Holland. Before the days of air travel it was a tedious, uncomfortable voyage by ship, across the Indian Ocean, through the Gulf of Aden, up the Red Sea, and through the Suez Canal. Before air conditioning as well, the trip through the tropics was miserable. I have no idea how long it actually took, but I thought it would last forever.

Throughout the trip, our father told us tales of Holland, a place much different, he said, from the land we had lived in. We had traveled in Indonesia, and there didn't seem to be much difference between one place and another so we could only imagine what we were coming to.

When we passed through Suez to enter the Mediterranean, he explained that we were now in Europe, but that didn't mean much either. We only knew we were living on a ship on a voyage that had no end. Then, everything was overshadowed by a radiogram from Semarang. Our mother had passed away.

Papa gathered us around him, and told us Mommy had been terribly ill for a long time, that now she was at peace, and we should pray for her soul in heaven. The moment was serious and solemn, but it was a mystery. Our mother had been gone from our lives two years already, half a lifetime for Toni, one-third for Jopy, nearly a third for me. Only I remembered her well, and except for the day of our final parting and the tubercular cough, my memories were fading.

As we steamed through the Mediterranean the ship caught fire, and for a while we were surrounded by confusion and fear. The crew extinguished the fire, but we had to dock at Corsica for repairs. I have no recollection of how long that took, but underway again we sailed into the Atlantic, and up the European coast to dock in Rotterdam. The voyage without end had finally come to a close.

We boarded a train to the city of Oldenzaal, our father's hometown, and were introduced to our grandparents. After a short visit, Jopy and I were shipped off to a Catholic boarding school in a place called Berg en Dall, near the city of Nijmegen. Our little sister, Toni, remained in the care of our grandparents.

Jopy and I stayed there two years, unpleasant years for me. My parents were gone, I was overwhelmed with feelings of loss and loneliness, and I couldn't understand why our father left us. Under the cold, strict discipline of the sisters I rebelled. My resentment manifested as misbehavior, and I challenged authority. Some of my mischief is good for a laugh today, but then it was deadly serious. Those two years were another period I thought would never end.

Liesje & Jopy at Boarding School – 1930

I don't know what our father was doing during those years, but in his travels he met a German woman, a nurse. Their romance was brief, in six weeks they were married. One day, Jopy and I were bundled up, and shipped to our grandparents' home. Papa was there with his new wife, and Toni was sitting on her lap.

Liesje & Jopy – Oldenzaal – 1931

We met our new stepmother, the visit ended quickly, Jopy and I went back to the boarding school, Toni returned to Indonesia with our father and his new wife, and my lonely days returned. I don't remember how long this second separation lasted, but one day we were packed up and sent back to Indonesia. I think the sisters were as glad to see me go, as I was glad to be free of them. Once more we traveled by ship, this time in the care of a steward.

We were reunited with the family in the city of Banda Aceh, on the island of Sumatra, and for the next few years I remember an idyllic life surrounded by the tropical beauty of Sumatra. But still we moved as our father was reassigned to different posts, Banda Aceh first, then Medan, and Padang.

Our house in Banda Aceh

I have a vivid memory of a holiday trip to the mountain resort of Lake Toba. It was cool there, in contrast to the steamy lowlands, and there were elephants loaded with great boxes of goods in transport.

At Lake Toba - 1932

Stepmother, Children, & a "dilemon," - 1932

In 1935, father was reassigned to the hospital in Jakarta, and there was another trip to Europe in 1936. I was fourteen. We visited our paternal grandparents in Oldenzaal, our stepmother's family in East Prussia and then went to Berlin for the Olympic games.

We girls stayed in the hotel while our parents attended the games. It wasn't the most thrilling way to spend our time, but there was a day of excitement when a military parade passed the hotel. We hung out the window to watch Hitler ride by on the street below, resplendent in his Nazi uniform, standing in his touring car and giving the Nazi salute in response to cheering crowds. We had no inkling then, but nine years later that hotel would be rubble, and Hitler would be dead, along with many of the crowd that cheered him.

Three Sisters – Jakarta – 1936

Through the 1930s, international tensions increased, and September 1, 1939, Hitler invaded Poland. Britain and France declared war on Germany, and the most destructive war in human history was on.

The war would have a profound effect on my life, but there was no hint of it then. In the tropical idyll of Indonesia, we weren't affected. Europe and its war were distant, a problem for people on the other side of the world that we knew of only through the hissing medium of short wave radio.

That year my father was still on active duty, and our family was living in Salatiga. I finished my formal education, left home, and moved in with my Aunt Toos in Bandung, to look for work. Through my years growing up, I had long hair I kept in braids. I wanted to cut it, but my father refused, a constant battle between us. The day I left, I gleefully sheared the hated braids, and never looked back.

My Parents – Salatiga, 1939

I found a temporary job house-sitting in Jakarta. The job was short-lived, but two events occurred that influenced my future. The absentee homeowner contracted for some electrical work, and I met the contractor, a young, single, Dutch electrical engineer named Ben. He invited me on a date, we became acquainted, and began the kind of formal relationship unmarried couples had those days. Eventually we became engaged.

Not long after we met, I contracted pneumonia, and underwent the long hospitalization usual in those days before antibiotics. In the meantime, my father had retired from active service, and my parents moved to Bandung. An old friend from my father's service days, a doctor who ran a clinic and a nurses training academy in Bandung, came to check on my condition. While he was there he offered me an opportunity to train with him, and when I was fully recovered, I went to Bandung to enter his academy. It wasn't a nursing school, as we know them today, nurses training those days was quite informal. We did practical work in the daytime, and attended classes in the evening.

I received a small stipend as a student nurse, but I was naive in financial matters. I found a dress I wanted, and blithely told them to charge it. They sent the bill to the clinic where I worked, and the doctor sent it to my father. I was in trouble. My income, a pittance, was enough for candy and soft drinks, and perhaps an occasional movie, but not expensive dresses. I was learning.

Nurses Training – 1940

Ben and I now maintained a long distance relationship. He owned a black Buick convertible with red leather upholstery, and would make the trip from Jakarta to Bandung to visit me.

In 1940, the Nazis invaded Holland. Our nation, too, was now at war, and the Dutch government fled to England. Still, in Indonesia, the war seemed far away.

February 21, 1941, I turned nineteen. I continued with my nursing training, and Ben and I continued our long-distance relationship. We set our wedding date for March 22, 1942, I ordered my trousseau, and made a reservation for our reception at the Hotel des Indes in Jakarta. Then our world collapsed.

CHAPTER II
THE WAR

December 7, 1941, Japan attacked the U.S. at Pearl Harbor, one of several coordinated attacks throughout the Pacific that included the Philippines, Singapore, and the Dutch East Indies. Japan turned all of Pacific Asia into a battleground as she sought the raw materials needed to sustain her economy, and fight a wide-ranging war.

Over the next two months the Japanese defeated allied sea and air forces in the Indies, and on February 21, 1942, my 20th birthday, they landed on the islands of Timor and Bali. The Dutch army, spread thin through the islands, poorly equipped, and soft from generations of easy garrison duty, fell quickly to the battle-hardened Japanese, many of whom had fought in Manchuria.

March 5, 1942, Japanese soldiers marched into Jakarta. In Bandung on March 8, two weeks before my planned wedding date, they captured the high command of the Allied forces in Indonesia, and formal resistance ceased. Thus began three and one-half years of Japanese occupation.

I had just turned twenty. I had endured darkness during the years in boarding school, but now, under the rule of the Japanese military government, began the darkest period of my life.

The next few months are a confusing hodgepodge. I remember caring for a burned, and blinded Royal Air Force pilot in the hospital in Bandung before the Japanese arrived. Sometime later I resigned from the clinic in Bandung, and returned to Jakarta, where I checked into a hotel for women that had been my temporary residence on a previous trip.

Our futures were uncertain, but my prospective in-laws wanted me to visit. Ben bought me a ticket to Surabaya where they lived, and I went there to meet them. I only stayed a few days, but in the meantime the Japanese military government instituted a system of travel permits. I needed one to return, and when I applied, the Japanese agent smiled, and said he would be glad to issue me one if I were to meet him at seven o'clock that evening. I never showed up, and in the darkness before dawn the next morning, I pedaled my bicycle to the station, boarded the train without a permit, and rode back to Jakarta.

As the Japanese tightened the screws, they first rounded up the Allied soldiers, and prepared to ship them to prisoner-of-war camps. My father, recently retired, was recalled to active duty, and captured with the rest. With the other soldiers in Jakarta, he was herded into a temporary compound in a park in central Jakarta. The compound was screened from public view.

One day I rode my bicycle past, and stopped to peek in under the screen. I recognized my father and my uncle among the prisoners inside, and concurrently received an introduction to Japanese rule.

While I was peeking, a Japanese soldier came up behind me, and jerked me upright. My bicycle crashed to the ground, and while I fought to regain my balance, the soldier held me and slapped me hard, three times, shouting, "Baka yaro," a Japanese curse meaning "Stupid Fool." My blouse was torn open, and as the soldier turned me loose I heard the spectators laughing. Profoundly embarrassed, I covered myself, picked up my bicycle, and rode away. I avoided such public humiliation in the future, but similar episodes were a daily occurrence. The Japanese were teaching us how things were going to be under their occupation.

When the soldiers were all captured, my father was sent to Hokkaido, in Northern Japan, a place of harsh winters, starkly different from tropical Indonesia. The prisoners there were used as slave labor to mine coal. Gone four years, my father was one of the few who survived to return. The uncle I had glimpsed, my Aunt Toos' husband, was lost at sea when the allies torpedoed the Japanese P.O.W. ship he was on.

When the military were controlled, the Japanese turned to rounding up civilians, first men, later women and children. They planned to single out the Dutch, and put them in concentration camps, but this was easier said than done. The Dutch had been in Indonesia nearly four centuries, and thousands of people had mixed Dutch and Indonesian blood. There were dark-skinned people with Dutch names, and light-skinned people with Indonesian names, and who, of whatever ancestry, would willingly identify themselves as Dutch if it meant imprisonment? The final decision was based largely on skin color. As a blue-eyed blonde with a Dutch name, you know where I went.

Civilian men were next after the soldiers, and my fiancée was taken quickly, though his Buick convertible was "liberated," by some Japanese soldiers even before they took him. When the men were accounted for, they turned to women and children.

Civilian camps were segregated by sex, separate camps for men, other camps for women and children. My family was separated, Mother and Toni in Bandung, Jopy in Salatiga, I in Jakarta, and my father a P.O.W. in Japan. For the next three-an-one-half years we had no communication. None of us knew the fates of the others, had we survived, or not.

All of us who were interned were uncertain of our futures. We hoped for humane treatment, but the record of history tells the story. There are many books by survivors that document the privation and brutality visited on their captives by the Japanese. The rest of my family experienced that suffering, my story is different.

I hadn't been in camp long when I witnessed an event that created a watershed in my life. My aunt Toos, a pleasant, attractive woman with long blond hair was in the same camp as I. We had been there only a few days when a detail from the men's camp was brought in to remove the garbage. Toos husband, my uncle Gerrit was among them.

Fraternization between men and women was strictly forbidden, but excited by the sight of her husband, Aunt

Toos waved to him. A guard saw her, and with a shout he dragged her away screaming. They lashed her to a tree, and under the horrified eyes of her husband and the assembled prisoners, they proceeded to beat her bloody, an object lesson of what would happen to those who disobeyed the rules.

The sight is burned into my memory. When I think of it today, her screams ring in my ears. I see her blond hair flying and reddening with blood, then her hair matted with blood as she lay moaning on the ground. My uncle Gerrit carried that image to his grave. He is the uncle lost at sea on a torpedoed P.O.W. ship.

I would not put up with such horrific nonsense. I was leaving.

I had made friends with a young woman named Betty, the daughter of a German father, and an Egyptian mother. As Japanese allies, Germans were not subject to imprisonment, but Betty was rounded up because she couldn't immediately demonstrate her German ancestry. We both wanted out. With no thought for the difference in our situations, and no plan for the future, we conspired to escape.

The camps, hastily constructed by the Japanese, were at first simple structures of wood and bamboo, surrounded by barbed wire, and guarded by sentries. Betty and I wandered through the camp probing for weaknesses, looking for any opportunity to escape.

We found a place where a gully ran under the barbed wire leaving a gap that was out-of-sight of the guards at times in their rounds. One moonless night we slipped out under the wire. We hadn't planned beyond finding shelter that first night; we'd deal with the future as it came. I had hoped to find help from one of my Indonesian friends, and to our good fortune, she took us in.

If I had thought things through, if I had any sense of what was to come, I would have had second thoughts, but I had turned a page. Escaping that camp was the biggest mistake of my life. It put me into survival mode for the next five years.

The first thing I did was to change my Japanese-issued identification card from "Dutch," to "Dutch-Indonesian." It meant changing the words on the card from "Blonde," to "Blonde-Indo." Then I dyed my hair with henna, and darkened my skin with makeup, to appear as a person of mixed race. The disguise was effective, but my forged I.D. was crudely done. I was stopped by the military police more than once. Each time my heart jumped up to my throat, but the I.D. was never questioned.

Our presence was a danger to my Indonesian friend, and we were pressured to leave. Betty found the evidence she needed to prove her German ancestry, and resumed a relatively normal existence. I had to hide. The danger of exposure and punishment was ever-present.

Some frantic contacts with friends found me a place to stay with a Timorese woman who took me in at some danger to herself. There are many ethnic groups in Indonesia, and the natives of Timor are primarily Melanesian, darker-skinned than the Javanese. Most of them are Christian, not Muslim, and they have a history of resisting authority. The Japanese seemed to pay less attention to them than other groups. I was safe as long as I kept a low profile.

In the beginning the Japanese were welcomed as liberators, but the natives soon found they had traded the yoke of Dutch colonialism for a new yoke, heavier still.

Shortages quickly developed as the Japanese occupiers drained the islands' resources to feed their war machine.

Hiding out, in constant danger of exposure, with no money, and no means of getting any, finding food was ever more difficult. I was desperate. Hunger gnawed at me, and I became gaunt. At the end, I was reduced to eating a sweet potato called "ubi," that I scrounged by raiding gardens in the night. I didn't always have fuel to cook with, and some days I had to eat them raw. My stomach churns today, at the memory.

Betty found work in a military store that catered to Japanese officers, and we kept in touch. She helped as she could, but as a non-Japanese, her own existence was precarious. In the oppressive environment of the Japanese occupation, her relationship with an escapee from a concentration camp endangered us both.

Today I wonder at her deeper motives, but she did something that resolved part of my problem, and set in motion a new train of events that changed the course of my life.

She spoke to me about the customers who frequented her store. One particularly she described as handsome, well mannered, and somewhat European in appearance. His name was Sakai, and he worked with the Japanese news agency, Domei.

One day Betty said she had told him about me, and he wanted to meet me. My experience had not generated kindly feelings toward any Japanese, and I was dubious, but her description aroused my curiosity. In my desperate circumstances I found no real reason to refuse.

Betty introduced us in February 1943, the month of my twenty-first birthday. Sakai arrived that evening in an elegantly tailored civilian suit. Slim, with warm, intelligent eyes, and dark, wavy hair, I thought he looked French. Courteous and handsome, with a calm, aristocratic manner, he was unlike the rude and arrogant soldiers and military policemen I encountered before. I found him attractive. Much later I learned the source of his manners, he was the scion of a noble family.

Sakai – 1943

Japan had a centuries-old aristocracy whose then current form dated from 1868. That year, forces loyal to the Emperor Meiji, defeated the Tokugawa Shogunate, a military dictatorship that had ruled Japan nearly three hundred years. The event restored the Emperor to the

Japanese throne, and that Imperial government ruled until it was dismantled after Japan's defeat in World War II.

The Shoguns drew their power from the Samurai class, in which the highest rank were feudal lords called "Daimyo," major landowners with many retainers. The Sakais were Daimyo with lands in Gumma prefecture.

The Meiji restoration established an aristocracy of different degrees, patterned on the British peerage, and the Daimyo were assigned titles according to rank. The Sakai family head was awarded the title, "Count."

Sakai and I were attracted to each other, and our relationship blossomed into a romance. He nicknamed me "Lily," after Lili Marlene, the heroine of a nostalgic barracks ballad popular throughout the world's armies in World War II. I carried that nickname for many years after, not always with pleasant associations.

We knew little about each other, and our relationship was fraught with danger. I was an escapee from a prison camp, and the Japanese army had strict anti-fraternization rules for its members. We grew ever more serious about each other and I became pregnant. This created a new set of problems unique to our situation.

Our relationship could not be open because of my escapee status and the Japanese anti-fraternization rules. Neither could it be kept entirely secret. Friends and acquaintances of both of us knew of it, and we could only hope the Japanese authorities wouldn't find out. In hindsight it's likely there was no secret, and the authorities kept hands-off because of Sakai's status.

Another element of Japanese policy created a frightening complication for me. Girl babies were irrelevant, but if a son were born from the union of a Japanese and a local woman, the child would be taken from its mother and sent to Japan.

Throughout my pregnancy I agonized over this possibility and then, on May 3, 1944, at 11:39 A.M., in a birthing clinic in Jakarta, I bore a son. I named him Roy. He was a lovely child, fair-skinned with wavy hair like his father's, but his birth filled me with dread. I could lose him under the Japanese policy.

It was quickly apparent our relationship & my pregnancy had been no secret. The afternoon of the following day, a black van of the Japanese Kempei-tai secret police pulled up in front of the clinic. An officer strode into the building and began to rudely interrogate the staff. In the back of the clinic, in bed with my son, I quaked with fear. The staff argued vehemently with the officer, and he left without searching the place.

They had managed to turn him away, but we knew for certain the Kempei-tai would be back. I knew for certain I was not going to give up my son, so at 3 o'clock the next morning we slipped out, Roy and I, and returned to the Timorese woman. Roy was not yet two days old.

That place wasn't safe either. I was known to the Kempei-tai, and now they searched for me actively. For the next seven months, my infant son and I were fugitives moving from place-to-place. By then the locals were disenchanted with their harsh treatment under the Japanese, and many people risked their safety to give us shelter.

The last person to help was a Eurasian woman, Madame Boerboom, a professional fortuneteller. She was kind and helpful, and cared for Roy when I was gone. I felt secure in her house, but it didn't last. Someone informed on me.

Early in the morning, December 23, 1944, I was up and about in my housecoat. There was a knock at the door, and without thinking I went to answer it. The black Kempei-tai van was stopped at the curb, and two uniformed officers stood in front of me. They told me I was under arrest. I resisted, and pleaded for my son, but they insisted. Madame Boerboom told me it would be wise to go, and promised to care for Roy. At last, they dragged me out, shoved me into the van, and drove me to Kempei-tai headquarters.

At first they put me in a holding cell with other prisoners, and for most of that day I fidgeted, full of fear and apprehension. In the afternoon they let me eat, and led me to a private cell. I began to relax, and at nightfall I slept.

In the middle of the night the lights snapped on, I was jerked out of bed, and rushed to a brightly lighted room, bare but for a desk, a chair, and a metal cot. I was pushed to the floor, and forced to kneel.

A Japanese officer sat at the desk while another soldier stood by holding a rubber truncheon he slowly beat into his empty palm. The officer spoke Dutch, introduced himself as Mr. Watanabe, and began to question me gently about the infant's father. He wanted to know if the father was Japanese, and his name.

I refused to answer, and the pressure mounted. They threatened, cajoled, and tried everything they could to coax a confession from me, but still I refused.

Watanabe lost his temper, and roared at me to confess. The truncheon came down, and the beater shouted, "Kono yaro," a Japanese curse. I was frightened before, but panic rose in me now. I knew what would happen if I confessed, so I gave them false names, Admiral Yamamoto, and every other high-ranking Japanese official I could think of. The beater cursed me, and with every answer I gave, the truncheon came down. I tried to squirm out of his way, but he followed, and hit me wherever he could reach, my back, my shoulders, and my breasts. I hadn't nursed Roy since the previous morning, my breasts were swollen, and milk spurted from them.

I fainted, striking my head on the corner of the cot. They threw a bucket of water on me to revive me, and the pace of the beating and questioning increased. In despair I cried out for my mother.

"No mama here," Watanabe snarled, and the beater struck harder. I prayed to God, and collapsed again on the floor. Another bucket of water revived me, and as I came to, the man who was beating me threw his truncheon on the floor in disgust, and stalked out of the room.

Milk still flowed from my breasts, and bruises began to discolor the places the truncheon hit, along with oozing blood where blows had broken the skin. Watanabe called two Indonesian guards who picked me up, and half-walked, half-dragged me across the gravel courtyard to the shower. They were gentle and sympathetic, but I collapsed again along the way. When I revived they allowed me to bathe, and moved me to an ordinary cell.

I'm sure the Kempei-tai already knew most of my secret, but apparently without my confession they couldn't act. I knew if I told the truth my child would be taken away, and Sakai, regardless of his status, would suffer punishment. Despite the pain and terror of the beatings, I never confessed.

I was left alone physically, but psychological pressure continued. Some days after the beating two men came in to check the condition of my bruises. One smiled evilly, saying, "I see you're healing nicely. When you're better we'll do it again."

Roy was still living with Madame Boerboom, and they let me nurse him twice daily. An Indonesian nanny brought him to me, and performed other errands, as well. I had gone to jail in my housecoat, now soiled after the beating, and she brought me a change of clothing. She brought food daily, too, delivered in a "rantan," a device that stacked several enamelware containers, each containing a serving of a different item; rice on the bottom, meat in the middle, vegetables on top, etc.

I was allowed to bathe daily, and I had to cross the gravel courtyard to reach the shower. One day I found a stub of pencil on the ground. The place was littered with scraps of paper and empty cigarette packages, too, and they gave me an idea. I picked some up, smoothed the crumpled papers, hid them in my cell, and began to write notes to Sakai.

The first time I wrote a note, I rolled it tightly, stuffed it in Roy's diaper, & asked the nanny to deliver it to Sakai. He replied with a letter delivered in the bottom of the "rantan," and we corresponded that way throughout my imprisonment. We were lucky the guards never searched Roy's diaper or the food container. When the pencil dulled, I scraped it on the rough concrete wall of my cell to sharpen it.

Sakai was struggling to get me released, but there was little he could do, his own situation was precarious. Then we had a stroke of luck.

February 19, 1945, not quite two months after I was imprisoned, Sakai was riding his bicycle on the street. A Japanese staff car flying a general's flag drove past, and Sakai recognized the occupant, General Yamaguchi. Both had attended Gakushuin University, a school reserved for sons of the nobility. The General had been an upper-class mentor to Sakai when he arrived there, and they had become good friends. Sakai was surprised to see the General in Jakarta; he was supposed to be commanding Japanese forces in the Caroline Islands.

Yamaguchi stopped the car, the men conversed for a moment, and the General invited Sakai to visit him in his quarters. There they discussed the war, and the General told him things were going badly for Japan. The Americans were advancing through the Pacific, the Japanese army was retreating westward, they had evacuated the Carolines, and it looked like Japan was losing the war. Sakai was shocked. This information had been kept even from the official news agency where he worked.

My situation was heavy on Sakai's mind, and he pleaded with his friend for help. The General had enough authority to intervene, and the Kempei-tai were ordered to release me. Late in February 1945, I was finally free.

The protection of the general's influence, plus the fact that Japanese control was slipping as the end neared for them, meant that at last we could live openly as husband and wife. March 1945 began five months of relative stability in lives that had been fraught with fear, stress, and uncertainty.

Sakai's residence was a house that belonged to an interned Dutch family, and for this brief period we had an almost ordinary family life. On May 3, we held Roy's first birthday party, and Sakai introduced us to his friends. One attendee was Sukarno, who was destined to be Indonesia's first president.

In August, after the atomic bombing of Hiroshima and Nagasaki, Japan surrendered, and now began another period of fear, stress, and uncertainty for us. The Japanese were no longer in control, political unrest was rising, crime was rampant, and there was no immediate evidence of a strong hand from the allies. Sakai was concerned for our safety, and decided to move us out of Jakarta.

The city of Bandung is in the mountains, about 175 miles from Jakarta. My parents lived there when the Japanese invaded. Sakai procured a Japanese government car, loaded it with our belongings, and had me don a trench coat and a man's hat. I sat in the back seat with Roy on my lap while Sakai drove us to Bandung. Today this exercise sounds like cloak-and-dagger foolishness, but in those unsettled times, I'm sure Sakai had a legitimate fear of my being recognized as a Dutch woman.

We went to my parents' house. Empty now, it had been stripped and vandalized, but it was livable so we moved in with our Indonesian maid, a middle-aged woman named Isa.

We were there for only a short period before the Indonesian revolution drove us out, but several things happened in that time.

British forces had occupied Bandung. Sakai was fluent in English, and obtained an appointment as an interpreter for them. The Dutch internment camps were being emptied, and my sister Toni showed up to stay with us until we were forced to evacuate.

Shopping one day, I felt a hand on my shoulder. I turned to find my former fiancé, Ben, recently released from internment. He asked how I was, and whether we should get together again. I told him it was impossible, I was married now.

He knew there were no Dutchmen outside the camps so he asked if it were a Chinese or an Indonesian. I shook my head. Two Japanese soldiers strolled down the street across from us. "Not one of those?" he asked. I nodded.

"That's all right, you can leave him."

"No," I answered, "I have a child."

He wished me well, turned on his heel and left. A few days later he knocked at my door. The maid answered, holding Roy in her arms. Ben stared at the boy intently, and asked if it was my child. Isa answered, "Yes."

"He's beautiful," Ben said, and then he was gone.

The Indonesian revolution was underway, and lawlessness increased. Life on the streets was ever more dangerous for us, and around the end of September 1945, we were ordered to evacuate. An international agency, RAPWI, "Recovery of Allied Prisoners of War and Internees," had been organized by the allies in the waning days of the war to care for the thousands of allied military and civilian personnel captured and interned by the Japanese. We loaded our family and belongings in two "dilemons," a kind of two-wheeled horse-drawn taxi, and headed for the RAPWI camp.

On our way we were stopped by Indonesian militants, and forced out of the dilemons. They told us that Indonesians were no longer allowed to work for the Dutch, and ordered the dilemons to drive away, taking the maid, Isa, and some of our belongings.

Stranded at the curb now, Toni, Roy, and I were surrounded. Toni said something uncomplimentary in Dutch, and one of the militants understood. They closed in around us, but a RAPWI truck drove up, and dispersed them. We climbed into the back of the truck, and rode the rest of the way to their camp. A few days later, Roy and I were flown to Jakarta in a RAPWI aircraft, a PBY Catalina. Toni went her own way in the camp, and I lost track of her

Liesje in The RAPWI Catalina.

In Jakarta after a few confusing days in another RAPWI camp, Roy and I were allowed to leave, and we moved in with Madame Boerboom again. Sakai stayed in

Bandung, interpreting for the British Army, and I heard nothing from him.

The Japanese army was dissolved, and the Dutch and British were trying to reestablish hegemony, but the Indonesian independence movement was reaching its peak. Sukarno had declared the nation's independence a few days after the Japanese surrender. The Indonesian people were ready to follow him, but the revolution was disorganized. Political instability increased throughout the countryside, except in the core of Jakarta where the British and Dutch armies were in firm control.

The old order was gone, and the times were dangerous, but still we had to live. Roy and I were living with Madame Boerboom, my mother was still in the concentration camp, now a RAPWI camp, we had not heard from Jopy, and Toni showed up again to take up residence with our mother. Sometime in October, my father returned after four years as a P.O.W. in Hokkaido. My parents were reunited, and I told my father about Sakai. He was bitterly disappointed, and opposed the marriage.

One day, riding with Roy in a dilemon, I met my parents walking. We stopped to talk; my father took Roy in his arms, and stared at him a long time. At last he looked at me, and said, "You have a beautiful child." We were reconciled.

I was worried about Sakai. For more than a month there had been no word, and I was anxious to hear from him. At last I received a letter, dated Nov. 1, 1945. He spoke tenderly to me, and told me what had happened to him. He was still working as an interpreter with the British army in Bandung, and asked me to join him. He was in good spirits, but his optimism didn't last.

The British began to move into outlying areas, but they underestimated the Indonesian drive for independence. They were under attack throughout the islands, and it was plain that they weren't going to stay in Indonesia any longer than necessary. Sakai recognized there was no future for him interpreting for the British army, and as a defeated Japanese officer, he had no vision of his own future. At least he wanted us to be with him.

Still in Bandung, separated from us, Sakai had been pondering our future prospects. On December 31, 1945, he wrote me a long letter. He advised that Roy & I should go to Holland with my parents, but I wanted to stay in Indonesia as long as he was here. He visited us in Jakarta several times, and met my father who was favorably impressed.

In early 1946, things had stabilized enough so the Japanese soldiers began to be repatriated. From the surrender until then, the defeated Japanese had wandered freely, but now they were herded into camps to be processed for return. Ships loaded with returning soldiers began leaving for Japan from the port of Tandjoeng Priok.

There were a number of "war brides," like myself who wanted to stay with their Japanese husbands, but regulations prohibited them from doing so. Sakai negotiated the matter with the authorities, and succeeded in having the rules changed. I could accompany him to Japan, if I wished, and that was my wish.

We discussed the matter with my father again, and all agreed this was the way to go. I was anxious. I knew nothing of Japan, but my father advised me to go ahead. If it didn't work out, I could return to Indonesia.

CHAPTER III
TO JAPAN

April 18, 1946, we three boarded ship at Tandjoeng Priok for the voyage to Japan. I was now twenty-four, Sakai was thirty-one, and in two weeks Roy would be two. My mother brought us a rucksack full of food for the trip.

The ship was crammed with returning soldiers, as well as a number of families like ours. There were ninety women altogether, most with at least one child. This was a cargo ship not equipped to carry passengers, so we had to sleep atop cargo in the hold. Steaming northward, we stopped often along the way to take on more soldiers, or discharge cargo. Leaving Singapore, we ran into a typhoon with heavy seas that lasted several days.

Fear and seasickness descended on us all. I was still nursing Roy, and my resistance was low from the years of stress, and poor food. Unable to keep food down, I lost weight. Our accommodations were crude and cramped, and to all the families, the trip seemed endless. After three miserable months we finally reached Japan.

Mid-July, 1946, we docked in Nagoya, and had our first look at the defeated nation. The crowd at the ship's rail stood silent as we viewed the devastation before us. The port had been heavily bombed. It appeared as though everything was destroyed. The few people about were poorly clothed, with somber faces reflecting the shambles around them.

As the families disembarked, we were herded into a bombed-out aircraft hangar. They sprayed us with DDT, ordered us to take showers, then served us our first meal in Japan, a ball of rice, a cup of miso soup, and a pear. I shared mine with Roy.

We camped in that bombed-out hangar two days while they completed our processing. On day three we boarded a train for Tokyo.

The ship was bad, the train worse. Packed so tight with returning soldiers we couldn't move, hot and humid in the dead of summer, the air was sharp with the stench of unwashed bodies. We couldn't view the scenery, or examine the countryside we passed through; the train was too full. Thankfully the trip only took one day.

We left the train at Tokyo Station, and my first impression was the heat. I was used to the tropical heat of Jakarta, but the humid Tokyo air felt heavy and oppressive. There was a stench in my nostrils, and I didn't know if it was something in the air, or the residue of our daylong train ride.

The stench was in the air. In those food-short days, a Japanese staple was a kind of fish that had been dried to a leathery texture. Every day, a million mama-sans roasted those leathery tidbits on charcoal hibachis outside their front doors. It created a smoky, evil-smelling pall that hung over the city day and night. The stench never totally dissipated, and it's one of my lasting impressions of Japan.

Tokyo Station – Postwar

Tokyo station, an architecturally attractive brick structure, originally had two impressive domes flanking a peaked roof. The domes and interior were destroyed in the firebombing in 1945, leaving the masonry shell. A year after the bombing now, reconstruction had begun. Originally three stories, the station had been shortened to two, and the domes replaced by angular, peaked roofs. The interior restoration was incomplete, and Sakai caught his breath as we stepped off the train to see the fire-blackened interior walls of the burned-out station.

The view down the boulevard in front of the station was pleasant. Modern office buildings flanking the boulevard seemed intact, but older buildings of masonry construction were burned-out, their roofs gone, empty windows gaping in the brick walls. In this central area, rubble from the destruction had been cleared, and some of the buildings were in use by the Allied occupation forces. The Imperial Palace grounds, a few blocks directly ahead, had been spared in the bombings, and beckoned with park-like serenity.

The Imperial Palace Grounds

Sakai knew of the air raids, but even though this part of the city was being restored, he was staggered by the destruction. The worst was yet to come.

Deposited in front of the station with our meager belongings, our hearts were in our throats. Filled with foreboding, we had no sense of our future. Sakai searched for a taxi to take us home, but there were no taxis. He found a private car with a driver, and bribed him to take us to the Sakai family home in Honjo. On the way, Sakai fell silent. The devastation outside the central district was complete.

The streets had mounds of rubble piled down the central thoroughfare with narrow pathways open on each side. Every neighborhood had its public bathhouse, but only their chimneys remained, and there were many two-story concrete vaults with tile roofs and steel doors like a safe. I never learned what they were, but most neighborhoods seemed to have one.

Everything else was flat, a moonscape of rubble and occasional shacks made from fire-scorched sheets of corrugated iron. Here and there, salvaged roof tiles were stacked beside the curb, pitiful signs of hope, perhaps, that someone was planning to rebuild.

The people we saw were, like the ones in Nagoya, poorly dressed, with vacant eyes, and drawn faces, human beings as devastated as their physical surroundings.

Standard attire for men seemed to be worn bits of military uniforms, or threadbare business suits. Most of the women wore "mompei," a kind of loose and baggy trousers, topped by a baggy blouse. There was no color. Everything was drab.

Nothing was familiar to Sakai in this bizarre landscape. Nothing was left of the place he departed with a light heart four years before, one with his nation's ambitions of conquering the world.

We came to the place of his home, but it lay in ruins. Reluctantly he emerged from the car, and wandered over the grounds. Here and there were scorched fragments of broken porcelain, and twisted pieces of metal that had been hardware, or household utensils. No hint remained of the gardens that surrounded the house, nor even the footprint of the house itself. Weeds were the only sign of life. Disconsolate, he stooped to pick up a piece of rubble, and brush off the dirt and ashes. When he stood, the devastation in his face matched the devastation of the city around us.

Here were the ruins of the mansion built on the site of his ancestors' "Edo-yashiki." It held his family history and its treasures. It had been his home, the place he grew from child to man, but it was no more. He squatted down, covered his eyes, and wept.

In the time of the Shoguns, Tokyo was known as Edo, and the Daimyo were required to practice a custom called "Sankin-Kotai." Each Daimyo maintained a castle in his home province, but he also had to keep a residence in Edo, an "Edo-yashiki." His family was required to live there permanently, and the Daimyo himself had to spend every other year there, returning in the odd years to manage his country estate.

The ostensible purpose of this annual exchange was for the Daimyo to serve the Shogun's needs for support in Edo. In reality it kept them broke and off balance so they couldn't plot revolution or resume their feudal wars. The families' full-time residence in Edo made them full-time hostages as well.

Before the Meiji Restoration the Daimyo competed to display their wealth and power, and the annual Daimyo processions to and from Edo were grand spectacles led by banners, and accompanied by armies of warriors, bureaucrats, footmen, and laborers. When a Daimyo castle was far from Edo, the procession could take weeks. They were an expensive exercise that indeed prevented the Daimyo from diverting resources to war or rebellion.

The Sakai family was of a class called "Fudai Daimyo," a term that identified families who had served the Shoguns from the beginning. Over the centuries, many Sakais had been officials in the Shogunate government.

With the Meiji Restoration, the military power of the Daimyo was curtailed, but they retained aristocratic titles and personal wealth, including the "Edo-yashiki. Sometime in the early twentieth century, in the custom of the time, the ancient Sakai residence was rebuilt in the Western style. Sakai grew up there. It was the only home he knew, but now it was gone.

We had enjoyed a brief period of euphoria in the weeks after I was released from the Kempei-tai prison, but since then, as the war wound down, with every obstacle we confronted, Sakai had seemed to shrink a little. As he wandered the ruins of his home, I sensed a change in him. The confidence he displayed in Indonesia was gone. He was deflated, as though the heart had gone out of him. He had been rooted in this place, and his roots were destroyed. From that day, I never again saw the strength and sureness he displayed in Indonesia.

We had nowhere to go now, no resources, and a family of three to provide for. I had no thought of what we might do, no knowledge of this place, or how we might survive in it. I knew only that we had to live, and that he was responsible to provide for us.

We were two people raised with servants, one trained to rule, not to work, both tempered to some extent by our struggles to survive in the topsy-turvy culture of war, but neither of us experienced in the normal daily struggle for life in the working world, let alone in a war-devastated country, its people barely surviving. We were in trouble. We had no experience, no prospects, only our inner resources, and our will to survive.

Sakai had an aunt who lived in Kichijoji, a district that had escaped the bombing. He took us there, and she told us the rest of the family had returned to the ancestral home in Gumma Prefecture. She offered to let us stay with her, but the food shortage was severe, and Sakai was concerned about imposing. After two days in Tokyo, he decided to take us to Gumma.

We boarded the train at Tokyo Station, and headed out to the countryside. For the first time, I saw a part of Japan that wasn't devastated. It was much like Indonesia, with paddy fields, bamboo forests, and scattered farming hamlets. The rice paddies made a lush green carpet, serene as a painting. The moonscape that was Tokyo might have been on another planet.

The rural countryside was peaceful, but I was apprehensive. I had yet to meet Sakai's family, and the prospect filled me with dread. He assured me that they would welcome me as his wife, but there was so much strangeness in our situation, I was unsure.

As we pulled into the station in Isesaki City, there was a crowd on the platform. More than fifty people, family, friends, and local dignitaries, had turned out to welcome the return of the son of their local lord.

I stood in openmouthed surprise. I knew my husband had some background, but I never expected anything like this. The attention flowed to him, except a few curious, and perhaps disapproving, glances at me. As a woman I was unimportant, as a foreign woman, a curiosity. I later wished they would continue to ignore me.

I had arrived in a place where modern Japan had not penetrated. These were people steeped in the old ways of respect and reverence for their presumed superiors. In 1946, less than eighty years after the Meiji Restoration wrenched Japan from feudalism to a centrally governed industrial society, these country folk still lived, and farmed, and believed as they had for generations.

I was the first European many of them had seen, and probably the first to enter their community. I became not just another person, but a curiosity to be stared at, followed, and discussed in a language I didn't understand. I wasn't sure their attentions were friendly. I was, after all, one of the people who had handed Japan its first military defeat in history. I was uncomfortable, and a little frightened.

The Meiji Restoration was aimed at subduing the Daimyo and their warlike ways, and that included destroying the Daimyo castles. The Sakais, as others, suffered that destruction, and the place where their citadel stood was now a cherry blossom park, still surrounded by a moat filled with golden carp.

The family home stood outside the former castle grounds. A big house, and old, built in the traditional Japanese style with tatami mat floors, shoji screens for room dividers, and wooden sliding doors to close the outside at night, I found it interesting and novel.

They introduced me to the family. Sakai's elder brother, the Count, was there as was his widowed mother, a younger sister, and an eighty-two year old grandmother they called, "Baba-chan." Another sister was married, and living elsewhere.

Sakai was the second son. His father died in 1942, and his older brother inherited the estate, and the noble title. The Count was a stern man, visibly displeased with the shame of his younger brother's marriage to a despised "gaijin" (foreigner). His hostility toward me was palpable. My discomfort increased.

I had come into a family with a proud lineage, steeped in the traditions of centuries past, bound to a strict code of manners and conduct. My husband had violated that code by the very fact of marrying me. My own upbringing was in a colony whose manners and customs were even more relaxed than those of continental Europe, a society without rules in the eyes of the Samurai. It was going to be difficult to conform, but I was determined to learn, and to please them.

We went to the prefecture office to register our marriage and Roy's birth, and our names were entered in the Sakai family register. This legitimized our marriage, but the formality would prove a stumbling block when the marriage crumbled.

I was ready to settle down, and begin a new life in a new society with new rules, but it wasn't going to be easy. I was learning Japanese, but when I tried to speak, people tittered, covered their mouths with their hand, and turned away.

My mother-in-law gave me a kimono, a "yukata," a light cotton garment worn in summer. I loved its colorful pattern of blue and red morning glories. When I put it on, she showed me how to tie it, and how to wear an "Obi," the broad sash traditionally worn with the kimono. I was pleased with the way I looked.

Roy was a few months past his second birthday, and he also had a "yukata," but in the striped pattern traditional for little boys. We went for a walk together, and as we walked, we found ourselves at the head of a procession. The further we walked, the longer grew the procession. Perhaps the people were merely curious, but I felt they were mocking me. It happened every time I went out, and soon depression set in. I didn't want to go out any more. My new community was rejecting me, and I began to feel isolated.

Liesje in Kimono – Isesaki –1946

I could only talk to Sakai about this, and I complained to him that I would always be an outsider subject to curiosity and ridicule. He soothed me, counseled patience, and assured me that in time they would come around. As time went on I saw no progress, and I keenly felt his family's rejection of me. I was a fish out of water.

He showed little sympathy for my concerns, and our arguments increased. One day we had a serious quarrel. In anger, I took out our marriage certificate, tore it up, and threw the pieces in his face. I told him I had written my father for money to return to Indonesia. He was livid, and demanded I apologize. I refused. He knocked me down, and began choking me.

I saw through the open door that people were jostling for a better view of our fight. I feared for my life, I apologized, and he released me. He had done what his culture demanded, and controlled his wife, but I felt the same humiliation I felt when the Japanese soldier threw me from my bicycle, and when the Kempei-tai beat me.

That wasn't the first, and it wouldn't be the last time he used violence against me, and I didn't realize it then, but that fight marked the beginning of the end.

It was plain that things weren't working out, and Sakai began seek an alternative. It was a dilemma. Starvation stalked the cities, while here in the countryside there was no shortage of food. But we were city people, neither of us attuned to country life and the old ways. Furthermore, my state-of-mind would not permit us to stay any longer in his brother's keep. We decided to return to Tokyo.

We stayed in the village about three months, and left shortly before winter set in. In Tokyo, Sakai found a rental on the first floor of a mansion in Azabu, another area that escaped the firebombing. The Soviet embassy was right across the street.

Relieved from the constraints of his brother's household, we were determined to make a new life for ourselves, but most of Tokyo had been destroyed, and the economic system was in tatters. Most people were in desperate circumstances living hand-to-mouth, and the nation was under control of the Allied occupation forces. The question we faced was how to make a living.

Sakai had money, and we bought a grocery store in Ginza, Tokyo's main shopping district. At that time, Japanese were forbidden to open new businesses, but my status as a foreign national allowed us to do so. Sakai used this permission to buy the store, and began selling fish there. He called the shop, "Lily May." I was to stay home and take care of Roy.

Selling fish was a practical idea, people always have to eat, and there was little food available. But Sakai had no experience in business, nor did I, and anyway, for the Samurai, commerce, agriculture, and manufacturing, are pursuits for lesser folk. For them, socially acceptable endeavors are intellectual pursuits, art, music, poetry, writing, etc., and Sakai was the quintessential Samurai.

Ordinary Japanese have a short saying which means, in essence, that the amateurish business endeavors of the Samurai always fail. Sakai proved the adage. The shop was bankrupt in three months.

In university, Sakai had planned to become a writer. He had done some writing before the war, and in Indonesia he had been an editor for the news agency, Domei. He began to write again, but he had no literary history, no connections. Even writers with reputations were unemployed. Sakai couldn't sell his manuscripts. Writing wasn't going to provide our living either.

We had to eat, and there was rent to pay. I thought of looking for work in the Japanese economy, but without Japanese language skills or any occupation, it was fruitless. I did have language skills in Dutch, Indonesian, and to some extent, English, and I found a clerical job in the Dutch Embassy. It was near where we lived, and I was able to care for Roy, but the salary was too low to support a family of three.

I began to look for other work. I was trained in nursing, and I heard the British Commonwealth Occupation Forces had a hospital at their headquarters in the Ebisu district. I went there, and presented my qualifications to the camp commandant. He hired me on the spot. The salary was enough to support us, but I had to work the night shift, and it was a long streetcar ride from Azabu to Ebisu. The area wasn't safe at night so Sakai would escort me to and from our nearest streetcar stop at Roppongi.

The stop was in front of the Finance Building, a former Japanese government building used then by the American Army for offices and barracks. One day I wore a colorful dress, and as we waited for the streetcar some soldiers watching out the windows whistled at me. Unfamiliar with the propensities of young American males, I innocently turned around to look. Sakai slapped me so hard my ears rang, and I didn't know why. Stunned, I cried out, and turned to look at him. He was livid with rage, and castigated me for wearing the attractive dress.

This was the fourth time I had been so publicly humiliated by Japanese men, once by the Japanese soldier on the street in Jakarta, once by the Kempei-tai who beat me so brutally, and now twice by my own husband. He was no different from the rest, and a hatred for him began to grow in me.

I met an older Dutch woman, long a resident of Japan. Her name was Nora. Married to a Japanese utility company executive, she had grown children. She was clerking at an American Army Post Exchange, a P.X.

If you ask why the middle-aged wife of a high-level executive was clerking in a retail store, the answer is simple. Those were hard times. Japan's economy was broken.

Nora lived in a fine country house, but her husband's livelihood was destroyed. Like nearly everyone those days they did what they had to, in order to survive.

Nora was older, and motherly. I confided in her about Sakai's inability to provide, and my difficulty in making a living for my family. She suggested I apply for work at the P.X. I did so, I was hired, and this became another step upward.

The salary was only a little more than what I was earning, but it was day work, and it carried a fringe benefit of incalculable value. I was entitled to three meals a day in an American military mess hall.

There were terrible food shortages in Japan then, and people were on the verge of starvation. All food was rationed, the rations were small, and there was little variety. With this fringe benefit I ate well, and could bring some of my food home to feed Roy. That left most of three rations to feed Sakai. Compared to the majority of city Japanese, we three were now eating well.

There was an element of danger in my good fortune. The P.X. held a cornucopia of American goods, and I could buy small amounts for my own use. Anything more than bare necessities was practically nonexistent in the Japanese economy, and there was a thriving black market in which American merchandise would return many times its cost.

Sakai became friends with a part-Indonesian man who was well versed in working the angles to make money. Sakai gave him some of the things I brought home, the man sold them on the black market, and returned a handsome profit. This began as a single event, but Sakai couldn't resist the lure of easy money.

I couldn't buy every day, and I couldn't buy large quantities, but Sakai pressured me to bring home more. The practice was illegal, it put my job in jeopardy, and I sensed a larger danger in what we were doing, as well. I wanted to stop, but it was hard to refuse him.

I was becoming ever more certain that we weren't going to make it together. His increasing brutality, his insensitivity to my concerns, and his inability to find a positive personal direction, were driving us apart. I told him I wanted to leave, he objected, and his hand came down again. I moved out of the house in Azabu.

This was late June 1947. We had been in Japan just about a year, I had been unable to accommodate to life with his ancestral family, he had tried two moneymaking schemes, failed, and given up, and I had held three jobs that barely kept us fed and sheltered. He had shown a growing capacity for cruelty, and my love was gone. I saw no future.

That month began another year of tumult and confusion for me. So much happened in my life, and the lives of those around me, that I cannot recall the precise chronology, but here are some things that happened.

I had become acquainted with a young woman, the daughter of an Englishwoman, and a retired Japanese diplomat. Her name was Joan. She offered me shelter, and I moved into a small Japanese-style room with a tatami mat floor. I had left Azabu with little more than the clothes on my back, so I slept on the bare tatamis under a single blanket.

Joan & Liesje – 1947

One day an agent from the U.S. Army's Criminal Investigation Division burst in, and searched my room, seeking illegally possessed P.X. goods. All he found was a British Army blanket I had been given by the British at Ebisu. Out of anger, my husband had turned me in, but for nothing. This was the last straw. It was really over now.

Two months passed. I was on my own, and making a living, but I missed Roy terribly. I worried about him, but I wasn't going to return to Azabu.

Once more I sought Nora's counsel. She advised me to simply go there and take Roy, and offered whatever help she could. I wrote Sakai to tell him I wanted to retrieve my personal belongings, and solicited help from the British commander at Ebisu. He offered to furnish a jeep with a British military policeman to drive it.

One evening in early September we drove to Azabu. Nora and I got out of the jeep and entered the house. Without speaking we went in, retrieved my belongings, loaded them in the jeep, and finally put Roy in as well.

Until then, Sakai watched silently, but suddenly he shouted, "Are you going to take the baby, too?"

He ran inside, returned with a pistol, pushed me up against a stone wall, and thrust the pistol in my face shouting, "Give me back the baby."

We were screaming and yelling, and Roy began to howl. Hearing the commotion, a guard from the Soviet embassy approached with his weapon ready. Seeing the guard, Sakai fled back into the house.

Roy With Soviet Soldier – 1947

We drove away, shaken by the violent confrontation. I was thankful for the Soviet soldier's intervention, it kept the violence from getting worse. I later felt compassion for Sakai for his loss, but at that moment I was only thankful I escaped an abusive relationship, and retrieved my son. Roy was three years old.

From the Japanese invasion, to my incarceration, to my escape from the prison camp, to the time on the run afterwards, to my dangerous clandestine liaison with Sakai, to Roy's birth and my fear of losing him, to the desperate months avoiding the Kempei-tai with him, to the painful time in the Kempei-tai jail, to the few idyllic months we had as the war wound down, to the disjointed months in Indonesia after the war, to the unpleasant voyage to Japan, to the trauma of our arrival in Tokyo, to the stressful months in the countryside, to our struggle to survive in Tokyo, to Sakai's abortive attempts to support us, to his increasing inattention and brutality, to my increasing alienation, to our progressive estrangement, to my decision to leave, to the trauma of the separation, and to my desperate act of retrieving my son, I lived in fear. Barely four years had elapsed, but in my struggle to survive there had been twenty, or more, discrete events, individually fraught with stress and danger. From the time of the Japanese invasion, there had been no stability in my life, no security. Fear followed my every waking moment. I was stalked by a malevolent fate.

In retrospect, those years are a small proportion of my life, but each painful episode seemed a lifetime. I had gone from myself, a naive young woman alone, to Sakai and myself, then to Sakai and Roy and myself, then to just Roy and myself.

That summer of 1947, marked a new beginning, but there was yet no prospect of stability and security. I still had to support my child and myself, I still had to find permanent quarters in a land with a desperate housing shortage, I still had to find care for Roy in a country whose language I didn't understand, and whose customs were strange and unfamiliar.

Other characters enter this drama now, subsidiary before because Sakai was my overriding influence, important now because they provided a framework of support I had lacked as long as I was with Sakai.

Nine of the women, who had been on the ship to Japan, were in Tokyo. We were not close-knit, but we were a sisterhood of shared experience who supported one another as we could. More than one had already separated from their Japanese husbands, at least one from the unpleasant surprise of being greeted at the train station by the husband's Japanese wife and children.

Most of those relationships, like mine, broke from the stress of survival in a foreign culture, in a war-devastated land, with no economic prospects. Few of us had emotional support from our husbands. Many of them, like Sakai, were adrift from the trauma of their defeat, and the loss of their social and economic anchors. Furthermore, most of them had reverted to their traditional cultural treatment of women. We were westernized, and we resisted the idea of total subservience, of always walking two steps behind.

Two of these women stayed with their husbands, one until his death from tuberculosis, the other through his life. Both played large roles in the next period of my life.

While I struggled with the separation from Sakai, other events were occurring as well. Sometime in summer 1947, I began working in the P.X. My manager was an Army Corporal named Roy Wilson. He was my husband-to-be, but I had no inkling of that at the beginning.

In quiet times in the P.X., Nora and I continued to discuss my problems, one of which was how to sever the legal ties that bound me to Sakai. Neither of us knew how this might be done, but to the Roy who was my supervisor, it was obvious I needed the services of an attorney. Neither Nora nor I, had any idea as to how we might find one, but one day this Roy presented me the business card of a Japanese attorney who advertised he spoke English.

The presence of two Roys in this tale creates confusion so I'll change their titles to what later became their standard descriptors among our friends and acquaintances, "Big Roy," and "Little Roy."

Another problem that plagued everyone but the occupation forces those days was lack of transportation. Japan had a sophisticated system of public transport that was one of the first things they addressed in their postwar recovery, but much equipment and infrastructure had been destroyed in the bombings. Local service was limited except in central Tokyo.

There were taxis, but their numbers were few, their range of operation short. Many were 1930s-era American cars converted to run on a gas generated by a wood-burning furnace mounted on the back of the car. They lacked power, were slow, and broke down frequently.

The Americans, on the other hand, had a military taxi service using Army jeeps with Japanese drivers. An American could call the motor pool, and shortly a jeep would arrive that would take him wherever he wished in the city. As a non-American that service was denied to me, but it was available to Big Roy.

It was hard to get around, and I had a lot of places to go as I struggled with putting together a new life. Big

Roy, more than once helped by providing me a taxi jeep, though I couldn't occupy it without an American present. Consequently, we spent a lot of private time together as the jeeps he provided carted me around. In this period he also accompanied me to the attorney, and was able to articulate clearly what I needed. The attorney took over, and the divorce was final in January 1948.

My other problems were more serious than just loose ends. I still had to find permanent quarters, and I still had to arrange for Little Roy's care.

So much was happening, I'm sure I'll miss the precise chronology, but I'll recount the next eight or nine months as best I can remember.

I had imposed on my half-British, half-Japanese friend too long, and I had to move. One of my Indonesian friends now began to play a significant role. Her name was Amanda. She was nicknamed Nelly, though I never understood the connection.

Nelly & Liesje – 1947

Nelly was an entrepreneur in the purest sense. A bold, assertive woman who disguised a steely character with a gentle, obsequious manner, she was a friend always, indeed my best friend through those years, but a friend who never took her eye off the dollar, or rupiah, or yen, as the case may have been. Her later life would be a different story, but those days I never saw her do anything that didn't turn a profit.

Nelly had a husband, and a child who still resided in a camp that had been set up for Indonesian repatriates in Tsuchiura, a town some distance outside Tokyo. She had somehow wangled an apartment in a bomb-damaged building in Tokyo, a single room with a toilet down the hall. It wasn't big enough to accommodate her family, so she spent the week in Tokyo working and doing business, and returned to Tsuchiura on weekends. The apartment could accommodate one more, and she invited me to move in and share the rent. It was a partial solution to my problem, but there was no room for my son.

There were no day care centers then, only orphanages that cared for parent-less children who had survived the air raids. There were many such; people will sacrifice themselves to save their children.

One of my acquaintances, in equally desperate circumstances, had her child in an orphanage run by Catholic sisters in a place called Fujisawa about an hour by train from Tokyo. I took Little Roy there, and the sisters accepted him. I was able to visit weekly, but it wasn't working. The sisters told me he refused to eat, and he wouldn't associate with the other children. He was pining away. I had to do something else.

My circumstances were known to many of my customers at the P.X., and one of them, the childless wife of an officer, offered what seemed like an ideal solution. She and her husband would care for Little Roy until I got on my feet. I brought him to live with them, they were nearby, and I could visit him regularly.

This arrangement worked well for several months, and I was thankful for what I believed to be a temporary arrangement. Out of the blue one day the lady came in with a paper she asked me to sign. I didn't understand the legalistic language, and I begged for time to consider it. I asked Big Roy about it, he read it through and told me if I signed it, I relinquished all rights to my son.

This was a chilling revelation. I naively believed these people were helping me out of kindness, but it was now obvious they had other intentions. I'm sure their motives for the child were good, but they hadn't made their intent clear to me at the outset. I refused to sign, but they continued to care for my son.

This created more stress, and the situation was complicated by the fact the officer's tour-of-duty was ending, and they were leaving. I had to find another arrangement, but I had no alternatives. At last, the caregivers placed Little Roy with a friend of theirs, a Japanese-American woman who had lived in Japan since before the war. This was not what I wanted, but I had no other recourse.

Conditions in that immediate postwar era were indescribably hard, and I was frantically seeking a way to bring my son and me together as a family. Sometime in spring 1948, I found a glimmer of hope. I located an apartment in a private home in Tokyo's Shibuya district. It had two rooms, a toilet, and access to a communal kitchen and Japanese bath.

Concurrently, one of the other brides from Indonesia was in even deeper trouble than I. Her name was Marie, her husband was dying of tuberculosis, she had an infant daughter who was seriously ill, and she had no money. We formed a coalition of the desperate. I rented the apartment, we both moved in, I retrieved my son, and she cared for him.

In effect, I had kidnapped little Roy from his father eight or nine months before. When I allowed the American couple to care for him, they developed a proprietary interest in him, and instructed their friend I was not to have him. I kidnapped him again from the strangers who kept him now. Whatever they may have thought, none of these people, from Sakai onward, reckoned with my resolve to keep my son, and care for him.

For all his life until then, little Roy had not enjoyed the stability of an intact household, and indeed for much of the past year, he had been passed from pillar to post more like a commodity than a child. Now we had the prospect of staying together in modestly comfortable surroundings. We were not to be separated again, though the future would bring one more trial on that matter.

As I look back on the year after I left Sakai, I don't see how I surmounted the obstacles that piled on, one after another. They weren't the mountains and stormy seas that lyricists write about, that kind of trial was yet to come. This was slogging through a swamp in the dark, praying for daylight, and hoping you didn't sink in the quicksand.

Other characters, and other events contributed to this drama, and Sakai is not totally out of the picture either. Big Roy is a looming presence, seeming to be there to keep the train on the tracks every time it was about to go off again. His financial help made the difference in moving into the apartment, and bringing little Roy & I back together. Nelly is still a factor in the picture, as well as a confluence of other events that binds this tale into a whole.

Sometime the previous summer, 1947, Big Roy was transferred to another P.X. in the Old Kaijo Building in downtown Tokyo. Until then we had both worked at Washington Heights, an American family-housing project. The Old Kaijo was a hotel for female civilian employees, and coincidentally, Nelly worked there too, as a switchboard operator.

Old Kaijo Building – 1947

I mentioned that Nelly was an entrepreneur. Her switchboard operator duties certainly provided some income, but the job was really an entree' for her entrepreneurship. She did a thriving business in used clothing she bought from the women in the hotel. Slightly used women's clothing in modern styles brought a lot more money from the style-starved Japanese than it was worth to the women who discarded it. Her trade was not illegal; the occupation authorities were only interested in preventing black market traffic in new goods.

Not all Japanese were impoverished then, indeed, the Japanese had a derogatory term, "shin yen zaibatsu," meaning, "new yen rich," denoting people who had a facility for making lots of money, but no real capital. These were Nelly's customers, and she had a marvelous source of supply, a hotel filled with several hundred women with little to spend their extra money on but clothes. She made enough in less than two years to buy some land and build a modest house to bring her husband and son to Tokyo.

Sometime in late 1947, Nelly convinced me that I should join her at the Kaijo so I applied, was accepted, and changed my profession from retail store clerk to switchboard operator. At the outset I was still living in Nelly's apartment, and this allowed us to commute together when our schedules coincided. It also brought me into daily contact with Big Roy since we once again worked in the same building.

As he helped me wrestle with my dilemmas we had become close, but I was freshly burned from one relationship, and leery about commencing another.

I had come to rely on him heavily for emotional support as well as help in navigating my way through the crises that were still a part of my daily life, b**ut now** another crisis loomed. The end of his duty tour approached. He had enlisted for eighteen months to become eligible for G.I. Bill educational benefits, and would be leaving by March 1948.

This generated more fear and tension in me until the day he blandly announced he had extended his enlistment to three years. Most of his friends were short-timers whose only wish was to get out of the Army as quickly as possible. When they questioned him about his decision, his standard reply was, "Hey, I met this good-lookin' blonde, we're havin' a swingin' time, & I thought I could stand a few more months of it." I was glad he felt that way; he would be there at least another year.

Around the time he extended his enlistment, he bought a civilianized military surplus jeep, which eased his, and my, reliance on the military taxi system.

Big Roy With his Jeep – 1948

After I left Sakai, he tried hard to get us back together, but he was not rooted in reality. He still had no way to offer us the security we needed, and I refused to tolerate his cruelty.

He wrote me several letters. The first, in September 1947, spoke of depression, and suicide, and reflected his obsession with the shame of Japan's defeat. He had a romantic notion of redeeming himself by performing some great act of self-sacrifice to accomplish a greater good. He pleaded for our return, but I was unmoved.

Later, he wrote again, this time of a mystical experience he had in meeting an elderly Catholic priest he had known from his youth. The priest directed a home for "feeble-minded," children on an island in Tokyo Bay. Sakai was entranced with the idea of helping the priest in his mission. It represented just the kind of self-sacrifice he had envisioned in his earlier letter, and it promised us a house and a living in a place untouched by the war.

His romanticism epitomized the widening gulf between us. Both of us had privileged upbringings, but I knew the meaning, the value, and the necessity of work. He had been born to rule, and the concept of using one's own labor to produce something of practical value was foreign to his way of thinking. My feet were on the ground; his were in the clouds along with his head.

He was a lost soul in the trauma of postwar Japan. His world was gone; the peculiar culture of the Samurai no longer existed. I lived in the real world, and I saw no prospect of his ever coming down to earth.

I never felt anything but compassion for the Japanese people. Their country was destroyed, and they were destitute, often dying in the streets in those early days. I began to feel compassion for Sakai as well, for the particular severity of his loss, but it was nowhere near enough to bring us back together.

I needn't have worried about him. Around the time my son and I were at last back together, Sakai married a Japanese woman, a professional pianist with an infant daughter born of a liaison with an American officer who had since returned to the U.S. Sakai now had means of support by someone with an acceptable occupation, he was the master of his household, he could continue his writing and any other dilettantish pursuits he wished, and he had a little girl he would groom to become a professional entertainer which, in her adult life, she indeed became with significant success. Was this marriage, and what came with it, the self-sacrificing act he so much yearned for? We cannot know.

Through this period, Marie, who occupied the apartment with me, and cared for Little Roy, was experiencing her own tragedy, caring for a sick daughter, and waiting for her husband to die. I don't remember what illness her little girl had, but there was a clinic, or hospital especially knowledgeable about treating it. The problem was getting the child there and back, and Big Roy again stepped into the breach with his ability to provide transportation. He also took her to visit her dying husband in a tubercular hospital some distance away, to his cremation after he died, and then to retrieve his ashes afterward.

When these events had run their course, Marie was relieved of the pressures that had made our coalition necessary, and she had to find work. She had office skills, found a job with the Dutch Embassy, and planned to move. I had to find someone else to care for Little Roy.

A man came through our neighborhood peddling vegetables he grew in his garden. I asked him if he knew of anyone who might live-in for room and board, and a minimal salary. He introduced me to a rosy-cheeked young woman, about seventeen, an innocent country girl, for whom there wasn't enough work on her family's subsistence farm to provide her keep.

Her name was Akiko, and she turned out to be a jewel. Except for occasional bouts of severe homesickness, she was unfailingly good-humored. Though poorly educated, she was disciplined, and had abundant common sense. I could trust her with caring for the apartment, for marketing, and when Little Roy started school in 1949, she first rode with him all the way to his school in Yokohama, and back. When it was certain he knew what was expected of him, she took him to the local station, and retrieved him when he returned. It's hard to imagine a five-year old traveling that distance daily alone on public transportation, but that's the way things were. Little Roy was just one of many.

Akiko stayed with me from the time she arrived around the end of 1948, until we moved out of that apartment in January 1952. At the end we took her home to her village, and her family. We were amazed at how much she had accumulated from the pittance we paid her. She arrived in that rural village like a conquering hero, and I'm sure we were the first Europeans most of those country folk had ever seen.

We drove a long way on Japan's highways such as they were, shifted to country roads, then country lanes, and a last we navigated on a cart track between the rice paddies. Akiko's house was old, with worn steps and woodwork, and a thatched roof shaggy with age. These people were as poor as any I had seen, and I'm sure Akiko's treasures were appreciated.

From the time I left Sakai and went to work in the P.X., Big Roy had been a constant presence, guiding me over the rough spots, providing answers to difficult questions, keeping on when I was ready to give up.

Once past the traumatic year between my leaving Sakai, and moving into the Shibuya apartment, life acquired some stability. I had a job; I had round-the-clock care for my son, and the most comfortable and secure place to live since I left home eight years before. I hadn't sunk in the quicksand, I had emerged from the swamp, and dawn was breaking.

I had it good compared to many those days, but the future was murky. I still had the option of returning to Indonesia, but there was a revolution underway there. There was stability in my life now, but no permanence, and I knew there were changes yet to come. Now came the songwriters' mountain-climbing phase.

Big Roy had been in my life more than a year, taking me where I needed to go, cheering me when I was down, steering me away from potholes. We had become lovers, and were talking of marriage, but there were obstacles.

Liesje & Two Roys – 1949

I had been burned in one marriage, I was leery of committing myself again, and I was afraid of facing adjustment to another new country. It hadn't worked the first time. I didn't have the burning desire to go to America that many had, I yearned for the idyllic life of prewar Indonesia. I had just begun to experience independent adulthood when the war took everything away. In the six years since, there had been only tumult, insecurity, and fear. I had no wish for more of the same. I wanted to go back where life was comfortable. That was impractical, of course, that life no longer existed for anyone.

There was the difference in our ages, Roy was 19, and I was 26. I wasn't sure of the social implications of that, society expected the age difference to be the other way around. Those days, much more than now, social convention was important, and it we were expected to follow it.

There was the question of income. Roy had been promoted to Sergeant, and in postwar Japan, a small fraction of his income added to my own made the difference between hardship and modest comfort for Little Roy and myself. Could we live on his pay in America?

My friend Nora scoffed at the idea of marriage, arguing that I was much too old for Roy. Nelly, on the other hand, more astute, and worldly-wise than I, and not so bound to convention, urged me to marry him. She saw something in Roy and in our relationship that I didn't. She scoffed at my reluctance.

At last I went along with the idea, but getting from there to the altar was easier said than done.

This was Occupied Japan, under a military government. The American Army served as mother, father, God, and confessor to all Americans under its jurisdiction whether in uniform, or employed by the government as civilians. Every one of them, who wished to marry, had to obtain, "Military Permission to Marry."

Altogether this was not a bad idea. It made sure that finances were adequate, examined religious and personal compatibility, and also insured that the marriage complied with the laws of the home states of the individuals involved.

The latter was a problem for us in one respect. Roy was under twenty-one, and needed parental consent. Indeed I did as well. Under Dutch law then, the age of consent for me was thirty. My father reluctantly approved, Americans all get divorced you know, but Roy's parents denied him permission. They thought he was too young.

We had jumped through all the hoops, but it was for naught. I was depressed and uncertain again, and our relationship was strained. If nothing else, Roy is persistent, though, and we soldiered on. The end of his enlistment came, and he was not yet twenty-one. The man must have been in love; he reenlisted, and stayed in Japan with me.

January 1950, he came of age, and we started the approval process once more. We provided reams of documentation of my marriage and my divorce, of my parental approval, of Roy's financial condition. We had interviews by the chaplain, and medical examinations. The wheels of bureaucracy ground ever so slowly, but on October 20, 1950, the blessing came down from on high.

The Consul of The Netherlands Mission to Japan certified that there were no impediments to our marriage since I had been married, and divorced, and had obtained the consent of my father. An Army medical officer wrote that both Roy and I were "determined free from infectious venereal disease, active tuberculosis and other major infectious diseases." Chaplain Maury Hundley, Jr., Major U.S.A., certified he determined there were no racial or religious barriers to the marriage, that Roy had $2500 in the bank, and "The prospective bride and groom have known each other for approximately 3 years. They feel this has given them sufficient time to have their affection tested and they are capable of making their marriage a success."

In our application we certified that our marriage didn't obligate the Army to anything that wasn't already covered by Army regulations, that we had income, savings, and insurance, and that Roy was not engaged in any unusually hazardous occupation. Roy's company Commander blessed our proposed union, as did his Battalion Commander, and at last Bryan L. Milburn, Brigadier General, U.S.A., Commanding General, Headquarters, Headquarters and Service Command, General Headquarters, Far East Command, issued his blessing.

Our marriage was recorded in the U.S. Consulate November 1, 1950, and we were married at the G.H.Q. Chapel Center on November 18. Chaplain Hundley officiated. We celebrate that date as our anniversary.

There were other bumps in the road along the way to this event. Roy was a P.X. manager, and his P.X. was one of a chain that served all the military hotels and installations under General Headquarters, Far East Command. The whole system came under investigation for irregularities in the summer of 1949. Several Exchanges were audited out of their normal cycle, including Roy's, and irregularities were discovered in all of them. The subject managers were all charged with larceny, the charges laid by the head of the system, an Army Major who was under investigation himself on other charges.

We had little confidence in the military justice system, so for several months we existed under a cloud of fear and concern. Investigations by the Army's Criminal investigations Division were inconclusive, and a Board of Officers was convened to examine the entire situation. The

Board included professional accountants who ultimately concluded the inventory and accounting systems of the Post Exchange division were incapable of accurately disclosing the alleged discrepancies. With regard to Big Roy, their report contained the sweetest words we had ever read. It said the charges against him were, "unfounded and lacking in proof," not merely unproved, but unfounded. The Major was court-martialed on other charges.

By now the Korean War had started, and that became another source of stress for us. Roy had transferred to a desk job, but his MOS (military occupational specialty) was Infantry Squad Leader. The North Korean Army decimated the infantry divisions that first went to Korea, and replacements were drawn from Roy's unit. We waited for him to get orders, but they never came. Later, we found out why. Three days before North Korea invaded, they began pulling Roy's teeth to give him dentures. The Army won't send you to war without teeth in your mouth, and there was a medical hold on him.

He didn't get his dentures until sometime between Thanksgiving and Christmas that year, and we got married just before Thanksgiving. I married a man without a tooth in his head. Can you imagine? It must have been love.

We were married in the Chapel Center at 8:00 P.M., on a rainy, miserable evening. We enjoyed a nice dinner sponsored by friends, and the Army being what it is, Roy went on duty at midnight.

Our Wedding

By the time Roy got his dentures, the replacement pipeline was full, and his unit vacancies were being filled by the new replacements. There was now little likelihood of his being sent to combat.

We enjoyed a quiet few months of relative normalcy, but pressures were building once more. Roy should have ended his tour September 30, 1951, but I was pregnant, due to deliver in November. The Army won't allow dependent travel less than six weeks before, or six weeks after a birth. Our departure date was pushed back to at least six weeks after the baby was born, and daughter, Sandra, was born November 5, 1951. That meant end-of-December at the earliest, but there was another complication.

Exclusionary laws those days, prevented permanent immigration of Asians. Little Roy was half-Japanese, thus excluded from legally entering the United States. As far as I was concerned, Little Roy and I were a package. It was all or nothing, we weren't going to be separated again.

Once more Big Roy's persistence paid off. He found the only exception to the exclusion was to have a private law passed to cover only Little Roy. He wrote his Congressman, who agreed to sponsor such a bill. Over a period of several months, the Congressman shepherded the bill through the Congress, and on October 29, 1951, it passed. Private Law 394 - 82nd Congress, Chapter 624 - 1st Session H.R. 4567, AN ACT For The Relief of Roy Sakai, stated (in part) that for the purpose of the immigration law, Little Roy "shall be held and considered to be the natural-born alien child of Corporal Roy F. Wilson, a citizen of the United States." (The Congressman was behind the times on Big Roy's military rank.)

Private Law 394 - 82d Congress
Chapter 624 - 1st Session
H. R. 4567
AN ACT
For the relief of Roy Sakai.

Be it enacted by the Senate and House of Representatives of the United States of America in Congress assembled, That, for the purposes of sections 4 (a) and 9 of the Immigration Act of 1924, as amended, and notwithstanding the provisions of section 13 (c) of such Act, the minor child, Roy Sakai, shall be held and considered to be the natural-born alien child of Corporal Roy F. Wilson, a citizen of the United States.

Approved October 29, 1951.

GPD—83—20382

Incl #1

Private Law 394 – 1951

October 29, 1951, Big Roy had a son by Act of Congress, and a week later he had a daughter by the usual method; fast fatherhood, indeed.

We had surmounted all the obstacles, and we were good to go. I had long since obtained my Dutch passport, but there were still legal hoops to jump through. Sandra needed a passport, and there were immigration forms to be completed and approved for me and for Little Roy.

Big Roy had successfully pleaded for delays in his orders, but now the orders were cut, there could be no more delays. The paperwork complete, we boarded ship, a former luxury liner, the "LaGuardia," converted to carry dependent families. We sailed from Yokohama, February 23, 1952, two days after my thirtieth birthday.

EPILOGUE

That's the end of this story, but not of the whole story, it covers only a third of my life. Nonetheless, I'll end it here. The rest of my life, though not mundane, pales in comparison with the experiences of my first thirty years.

My later life has not been entirely moonlight and roses, but it has been infinitely better than what went before. I don't have enough time left to complete a full autobiography, but I'll present a précis of later years, and tell what I know of what happened to some of the other participants in this drama.

Another page turned during our trip to the U.S. "Big Roy," and "Little Roy," received new designators; "Roy Sr.," and "Roy Jr.," and I will use those designators from now on.

Unlike my reception in Japan, my husband's family accepted me. I had lived in an American expatriate community five years, and I accommodated easily to life in America. We had lean times during the remaining year-and-a-half of Roy's military service, and three years after that as he finished his University degree. A third child, our son, John, was born while Roy was in college.

After graduation, Roy began a career in the Federal Civil Service that took us to five states, ending in Washington State. He retired early, in 1977, as a result of policy changes wrought by a change in the national administration. He worked two more years teaching, and administering a university extension center, after which, in his words, he "quit working for money."

After returning to the U.S. in 1952, including our post-retirement years, we lived in fifteen cities in seven states. Since our marriage in Japan, we have occupied twenty-two residences: one boat, three recreation vehicles, three apartments, two manufactured homes, and thirteen separate houses. Eight of these residences, were rentals, the other fourteen we owned (most in combination with a mortgage company, of course). The majority of our lives, by far, has been lived in homes that we owned.

One of my wedding photos shows me standing before the altar, flanked by four women. Two more kneel in front of me. We are seven of the nine from Indonesia who ended up in Tokyo. One of us had married an American and already gone to the U.S., the other had wed a Dutchman, and was living elsewhere.

Indonesian War Brides At Our Wedding – 1950

The kneeling woman on my right is Nelly, my closest friend through those years, and the only one of us to remain with her Japanese husband. An entrepreneur, in later years she built a chain of restaurants in Japan and Indonesia, and operated an international travel agency with offices in Japan and Indonesia. She made a fortune, much of which she gave away at last.

Nelly visited us once here in Washington State, while attending a meeting of international travel agents. She invited us to visit Indonesia with the promise she would pick up most of the tab if we could get there by ourselves. We went there in 1993, she met us at the airport in Bali, handed us a thick sheaf of Indonesian currency, and an itinerary that included two or three days each at a series of luxury hotels on Bali, and Java. She accompanied us when we went to check into the first one, and I had a revelation.

Nelly seemed to be no more than a simply dressed elderly Asian lady, but as we climbed the polished granite steps to the open lobby of the first hotel, she was transformed. She seemed to grow and expand, and at the top of the stairs she paused, head high, to gaze around imperiously. In moments there was a shout from across the lobby, and a servant ran out to greet us, bowing and scraping.

Our friend was obviously somebody more than we expected. I imagine her travel agency was an important source of the hotel's income, and she wasn't afraid to remind them.

We enjoyed our Indonesian stay, though I found that truly, you can't go back. I was relieved when our plane took off to depart. Toward the end of our journey we discovered the reason for the inexpensiveness of our stay. Nelly, ever the entrepreneur, had introduced us as her U.S. representatives on a tour to evaluate Indonesia's finest hotels.

Nelly and I corresponded irregularly over the years, and we did hear from her a year-or-so after our trip. She promised to send me a leather jacket I had admired, but the jacket never arrived, and there has been no response to contacts we have made since. I doubt she is still alive.

Both of the kneeling women in the photo were my bridesmaids. The other one is named Vera. Nelly was a Dutch-Indonesian mix, Vera was half-Russian, half-Japanese, though she was born and raised in Indonesia. Vera had one child, and also left her Japanese husband. Much later she married an American, and immigrated here, but that marriage failed, also. Her son grew up bright and ambitious, to attend university on an academic scholarship. He became a wealthy international businessman, and supported his mother in grand style through her declining years. She died in 2004.

The woman with the turban on the left of the back row is named Jean. She divorced her Japanese husband, eventually immigrated to the U.S. on her own, and in later years married an American. We corresponded regularly, but I've had no response for two years. Her husband passed away first, she had no other relatives, and I suspect she, too, is gone.

The woman next to her is Vera's sister, Olga, who married a Japanese-American from Hawaii. We didn't correspond, but I had news of her from her sister, Vera. Both Olga and her husband are gone now.

The woman on my left is Marie, who lived with me and cared for Little Roy while her husband was dying of tuberculosis. Her sick daughter survived, and later Marie married an American man of Indonesian descent. They immigrated to the U.S, and she had two more children. That marriage also failed, and she raised her children by herself. She completed a career working for the Dutch government, and retired from the Dutch Consulate in Los Angeles. In her later years, she met and married a childhood sweetheart, and they settled in the U.S. Both of them are gone now, too.

The woman next to Marie on my extreme left is named Tina. She, too left her Japanese husband, and later married a Dutchman who worked at their embassy in Japan. I later heard they were divorced, she moved to New Zealand, and has since passed away. This is all secondhand information; we never corresponded.

The eighth member of the group, Louise, one of the two missing from the photo, remained with her American husband. She had a daughter from her first marriage, and another son later. Her husband completed a full military career, retired from the Army, and later retired from a second career as a candy company executive. We corresponded irregularly over the years, and visited them at their home in Michigan, ten years ago. We have since lost contact. Both were in poor health when we saw them last so they may be gone, as well.

The whereabouts of the last missing member was unknown to us for many years, but in the middle 1990s, we reestablished contact. They had returned to Holland from Japan, and later immigrated to the U.S. He had retired, and she was sinking into Alzheimer's. Nonetheless, we visited them in 1997, at their home in the Upper Peninsula of Michigan and once more a few years later. We continued to correspond. Her Alzheimer's followed the usual progression, and he contracted a serious form of prostate cancer. Our last correspondence was returned "unable to forward."

Roy, Jr. enlisted in the Navy in 1962, and ultimately went to Japan to meet his birth father. The meeting did not go well. Sakai greeted him at arms length, and didn't publicly recognize him as his son. Roy had made a great effort to meet his father, but at the end he was rejected.

Sakai and I were reconciled by the time Roy Sr. and I were wed, and in 1966, we sponsored the Sakai family's immigration into the U.S. His stepdaughter, Michiko, had become an accomplished professional musician. Her stage name was Michie Sahara. It was the height of the folk music craze, and she had achieved popular success in Japan, but they thought there were better opportunities here. It was also a time when several Korean music groups enjoyed popularity here, and she toured for a time with one of them. That fad ended, as did the folk music craze, and she did not find success as a solo act. Eventually she went into business. We kept infrequent though regular contact, and her mother told us she passed away, September 27, 2000. She was only fifty-three years old.

By the time Sakai and I separated, it was plain there were fundamental differences in our perception of the world. In later years, old resentments seemed to surface in him. His reactions were not always rational, and our personal contacts were sometimes confrontational. Eventually we heard that his behavior had become bizarre.

Throughout his decline, his wife Masako, and daughter Michiko remained steadfast, and he died January 23, 1985. He was sixty-nine years old. Perhaps he was never really able to accommodate to Japan's defeat, and the destruction of the Samurai culture.

Roy Sr. and I were close by, and attended his funeral. Roy Jr., on the other side of the continent, still smarted from his father's rejection twenty years before, and declined to come.

Roy, Jr. returned from his Navy service in the late 1960s, and after a series of short jobs, went to work for a country club in Maryland. He still works there after forty years. He married at age thirty, has three children and four grandchildren, and has lived in the same house long enough to payoff the mortgage.

Daughter Sandra, married at nineteen, and was widowed at twenty-five when her husband died of cancer. She remarried, and had four children, one of whom died in an auto wreck at age nineteen. She has three surviving daughters and four grandchildren.

Our youngest son married, had three children, and divorced after the children were grown. He has two grandchildren. Both he and his ex-wife have since remarried. As far as we are concerned, his ex-wife is still a part of our family, and we have good relations with his current wife, as well.

We have always been fiscally conservative, though we made a lot of moves during Roy Sr.'s working years, and we did a lot of pleasure travel, as well. We are free of debt, and live comfortably within our means. I have strong memories of hard times, the worst of which lasted from the start of World War II, through the 1940s. Since the middle 1950s we have enjoyed financial security, though there was little money for anything more than necessities until the middle 1960s.

Altogether, except for the rough beginning, and perhaps the number of moves we made, our lives have not been uniquely different from most American families. The trials and tribulations we have undergone through our married years are unremarkable. The part of my life I wrote about here was.

And that's how it is.

THE END

Printed in the United States
140744LV00007B/1/P